A Newbies Guide to iCloud:
The Unofficial Guide to Making the Move Into the Cloud

Minute Help Guides

Minute Help Press
www.minutehelp.com

Table of Contents

Section 1: Introduction

Are you tired of manually syncing contacts, photos, music and documents? Now you can leave the cables and cords behind! Welcome to iCloud, Apple's free wireless syncing and online storage service. iCloud makes syncing your contacts, mail, photos, documents and music effortless. In fact, with iCloud, no "syncing" is required—documents and media are all right there for users on every device. While the concept behind iCloud is straightforward, it takes a little tweaking and customization to really get the most out of this free service. And for users who are new to the Apple ecosystem, or unfamiliar with cloud storage, iCloud can seem like an entirely foreign world. Where do my things get 'stored'? What if I run out of storage space? What happened to my MobileMe account? Can iCloud really work with my PC?

This guide will take you step-by-step through the process of setting up iCloud on all your devices, including the iPhone, iPad, iPod Touch, Mac and PC. We'll walk you through the process of viewing and editing the same document across multiple devices without needing to email updated versions or sync changes. Plus we'll demystify iTunes Match, and help you get started uploading and streaming music across all your devices, including Apple TV.

What is iCloud?
iCloud is Apple's first major attempt to unify all its online-only storage in one platform, combining MobileMe and iWork. In the past, Apple users could pay an annual subscription fee for a MobileMe account to remotely store and access files. Apple also offered a free service called iWork.com, a virtual storage and sharing solution for iWork files. iCloud unifies these services into one, combining remote storage with automatic syncing, no cable required. Unlike MobileMe, iCloud is free to anyone with an iOS 5 device or an Apple computer running Lion, the latest operating system. If you still run Snow Leopard, you'll need to upgrade to Lion before you'll be able to use iCloud on your computer. iCloud provides the following services:

- Mail
- Contacts
- Calendar
- Bookmarks
- Find my iPhone/iPad
- iTunes in the Cloud
- Photo Stream
- Documents in the Cloud
- Automatic download and purchase history for apps and books
- Backup and restore for iPhone/iPad

Every iCloud account comes with 5GB of storage. For many users, this storage will be more than enough, as purchased music, app, books, TV shows and PhotoStream content does not count against the free storage quota. Additional storage can also be purchased as needed directly from your iDevice.

Whatever happened to my MobileMe account?

If you are a longtime Apple user, you may have a MobileMe account. Apple's paid sync service, MobileMe, has been seamlessly integrated into iCloud. While MobileMe is no longer accepting new users, existing users may continue to access their accounts through June 30, 2011. If you use MobileMe, you'll find that all of the services that you currently use are available with iCloud, aside from iWeb publishing Gallery and iDisk. Need help making the switch? We'll discuss how to make a seamless transition from MobileMe to iCloud in 2.X.

So, how do I get started with iCloud?

Already activated iCloud on your iDevice, but not sure how to make the most of its new features? Skip ahead to Section 3 and 4 to start learning about how to manage your documents, photos and music in the cloud. Are you brand new to the Apple ecosystem? Wondering how to get started with iCloud on your Windows PC? Keep reading for step-by-step set-up instructions in Section 2.

Section 2: Getting Started: Setting Up iCloud

2.1 iCloud on your iDevices

iCloud is part of the iOS 5 update for iDevices, including the iPod Touch, iPhone 3G, 4 and 4S, and the iPad. In order to get started with iCloud, your devices will need to be upgraded to iOS 5. If you've just purchased an iDevice, then you're fully up to date and ready to go!

How do I upgrade to iOS 5?
1. Make sure iTunes on your computer is up to date; you'll need version 10.5+.
2. Next, connect your iPhone, iPad or iPod Touch to your computer
3. Make sure your device is backed up
4. When you connect your device, iTunes will prompt you to upgrade to iOS 5; follow the on-screen steps to download and install the new operating system and you'll be ready to go!

How do I get started?
When you first turn on your iDevice, you'll be prompted to set up your iCloud account. First, you'll need to sign in with your Apple ID. If you don't have one, you can create a free Apple ID. Next, select the Back Up to iCloud" option.

If you skipped this step when you first set up your device, you can still activate iCloud. From the home screen, select the 'Settings' icon and tap iCloud.

How do I customize my settings?

Once iCloud is activated, you will want to customize your settings. Go to Settings -> iCloud to activate/deactivate individual iCloud services for Mail, Contacts, Calendars, Reminders, Bookmarks, Notes, Photo Stream, Documents & Data and Find My iPhone. Activating these settings will sync your information across different devices. For example, activating 'Reminders' means that your reminders are synced between your iPhone and your iPad, and will also appear on your iCalendar. Activating 'Bookmarks' means that the pages you bookmark in Safari on your desktop computer will also be bookmarked on your iPhone and iPad.

You can choose which services and apps to sync across all devices. For example, if you have Gmail, you may not care about syncing your mail accounts or backing them up; after all, Gmail does a pretty good job of that already. So you may wish to leave this option as "OFF". If you use Apple's Address Book on your computer for contact management, however, you'll definitely want to enable Contacts by toggling on the "ON" option. This will sync your contacts across all your iDevices, to Apple's remote iCloud website, as well as to your computer. Plus, your contacts will be backed up.

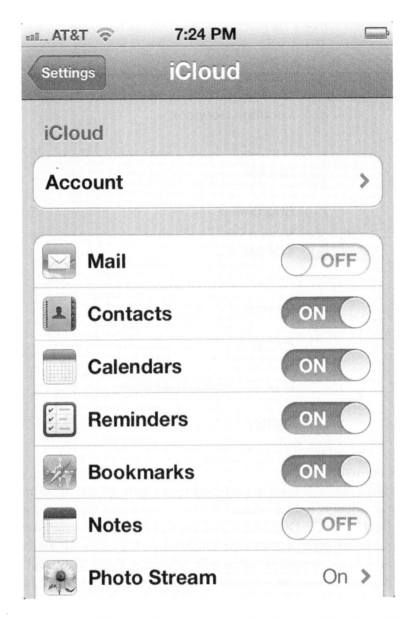

To activate iCloud's storage and backup features, go to Settings -> iCloud -> Storage and Backup; you'll need to scroll to the bottom of the menu to find this option. When iCloud Backup is enabled, iCloud will automatically back up your accounts, documents, settings and Camera Roll whenever your iPhone is plugged in, locked and connected to a Wi-Fi network.

How do I enable automatic downloads?
One of iCloud's most useful benefits is that all your content (music, apps and books) is automatically available on all your devices – without you doing a single thing. To enjoy this benefit, you'll need to activate automatic downloads.
1. Go to Settings -> Store
2. You can choose to activate automatic downloads for music, apps, and books

NOTE: To manage your data usage, Apple gives you the option of using a cellular data network (e.g., AT&T 3G) for automatic downloads. If you have a small data plan or just don't want to blow through your data allotment on a lot of books and music downloads, be sure this feature is toggled "OFF". You can still enjoy the benefits of automatic download anytime you are connected to a Wi-Fi network, such as at home or at work.

2.2 iCloud on your Mac or PC

Not only does iCloud sync with the apps you use everyday on your iPhone, iCloud also syncs with the same apps on your computer, whether you have a Mac or PC. Here's how to get started:

iCloud on your Mac
Before you start:
1. Make sure your Mac is running the latest version of OS X Lion
2. If you sill have Snow Leopard, you can upgrade to Lion by purchasing it from the App Store for $29.99
3. If you have Lion but are not sure if it is the latest version, go to System Preferences -> Software Update to check for any updates

Activate iCloud:

1. Go to System Preferences (Internet & Wireless) and select iCloud
2. Enter your Apple ID and select which services you wish to enable

Enable Photo Stream in iPhoto or Aperture
1. Go to System Preferences -> iCloud and ensure "Photo Stream" is turned on
2. From either program, click the "Photo Stream" icon in the left corner (next to Events, Faces and Places) and select the "Turn on Photo Stream" option
3. You can also manage Photo Stream within each program by going to Preferences -> Photo Stream (See 3.4 for more on managing Photo Stream)

iCloud on your Windows PC
Before you start:
1. Windows Vista SP2 or Windows 7 is required; be sure you are up to date on the latest version
2. **Download the iCloud control panel**

Activate iCloud:
1. Go to Windows Start -> Control Panel -> Networks & Internet -> iCloud
2. Enter your Apple ID and select which services you wish to enable
3. To access iCloud email, calendars and contacts, you'll need to have Outlook 2007 or Outlook 2010
4. To access bookmarks, you'll need Safari 5.1.1 (or later) or Internet Explorer 8 (or later)

How do I enable automatic downloads?
Whether you have a Mac or PC, you can enable automatic downloads through iTunes. Go to iTunes -> Preferences and select the "Store Preferences" option. Check which content you wish to enable, choosing between music, apps and books. (NOTE: from a PC, you'll need to go to iTunes -> Edit -> Preferences)

2.3 iCloud on your Apple TV

Many of the media features included in iCloud, including Photo Stream (see 3.4) and iTunes Match (see Section 4) are also available on Apple TV via iCloud. Music, photos and TV Shows can now be viewed on your Apple TV via wireless streaming from iCloud. Previously, users could use AirPlay or homesharing to stream video and music content directly from their computer to the Apple TV, as long as both the computer and TV were on the same network. Now, you can make a purchase at work and view it when you get home – no AirPlay streaming required. You can also view all images in your Photo Stream on your Apple TV, so that when your take photos of the kids on vacation, you can view them at home on your TV without syncing or uploading anything.

NOTE: Purchased movies can still be viewed via AirPlay, but are not currently part of iCloud wireless streaming. Only TV Shows and music can be streamed from your iCloud account)

How do I set my Apple TV up for iCloud?
Is your Apple TV new? The first time you turn it on and connect to the Internet, you'll be prompted to set up your iCloud account. If your Apple TV is not new (but still a second generation), go to the Settings option to update its software. Once the software update is complete, you'll be prompted to set up an iCloud account. You can change your account settings at anytime by returning to the Settings menu.

NOTE: iCloud does not work with the first generation Apple TV.

2.4 iCloud online

For MobileMe users, iCloud's online service will look familiar as it replaces the existing MobileMe online access. Even if you're brand new to accessing your data online, the streamlined interface mimics Apple's Mail, Address Book and iCalendar apps, making it easy to get started. Apple has purposely designed each app to function with a nearly identical user interface no matter what device (iPhone, iPad, computer, internet) you use the app on.

What is available from iCloud.com online?
The following is available on iCloud.com:
- Mail
- Contacts
- Calendar
- Find My iPhone
- iWork.

Information in these apps is synced directly from your computer and iDevices via iCloud.

Once you login to iCloud.com, you'll see the same gray linen desktop background and familiar apps.

1. To get started, go to iCloud.com and login using your Apple ID
2. Select an app to view contacts, mail, calendar or documents
3. You can also use the 'Find My iPhone' app to locate a missing iPhone or iPad (see 3.7 for information on using Find My iPhone)

2.5 Transitioning from MobileMe to iCloud

iCloud has replaced MobileMe, Apple's paid storage and sync service. Current users may continue to access their content through June 30, 2012. You can continue to access iCloud's servers from the web, just like you did with MobileMe. If you have a me.com or mac.com email address, you can continue using this account. You'll need to move any contacts, mail, calendars and bookmarks over to iCloud.

iCloud does not support iWeb – what will happen to my website?
Even after you make the switch to iCloud, Apple will continue to offer online hosting and publishing for any iWeb sites through June 30, 2012. You can continue publishing up to this date as well. However, you'll need to move your site to a new web hosting service if you want it to be accessible after June 30. In order to make the move, you will need to be running iWeb '09 and have a web hosting account with FTP support. You will need to move both your domain and website. Here's what to do:

Moving your domain:
1. Select a new host server and set up a new server account

---

2. Following your hosting service's directions on the hosting website, configure your domain; note the CNAME configuration
3. Next, go to your domain registrar's site
4. From your domain's registrar site, find the CNAME configuration
5. On your domain registrar's site, change the CNAME configuration from MobileMe to the new server; NOTE: It may take up to 24-hours for the change to be reflected
6. Sign in to me.com/account
7. From the account page, select personal domain
8. Click "remove domain" button to remove your domain

Moving your website:
1. From iWeb, choose Site Publishing Settings
2. Select the FTP Server from the Publishing drop-down menu
3. Enter the FTP information, including the FTP server address provided by your web hosting service, the user name for publishing to your web hosting service and password
4. Click 'Test Connection' to ensure the information is correct
5. Enter the URL for your website
6. Click Publish – your website has now been moved!

What happens to my MobileMe gallery?
You can continue using your gallery through June 30, 2012. However, you'll need to download and save copies of your photos to your computer. Otherwise, these photos will no longer be available after June 30.

I currently use more than 5GB of data for MobileMe – will I need additional storage for iCloud?
Yes and no. In iCloud, purchased music, app, books, TV shows and Photo Stream content do not count against the free storage quota. Depending on your storage needs, you may find that you do not need additional storage space. If you do, you can purchase more at any time directly through your computer's web browser or any iDevice.

Section 3: Content Management & Apps in iCloud

3.1 Mail in iCloud

When you set up iCloud, you will get a free ".me" email account. iCloud automatically pushes new emails to every device and keeps any organization folders in sync. While this is a nice feature, most users will already have a Gmail or an Exchange email account that automatically does this for them.

If you chose to use your .me as your primary email account, you can access it online via the iCloud.com website. If you are familiar with Mail on the iPad and Lion, then Mail on the web looks exactly the same. As far as web-based email goes, this is one of the nicest, most streamlined interfaces available. Plus, it's all ad-free.

In order to access your .me mail account, you'll need to enable Mail in your iCloud settings on either your iPhone, iPad, iPod Touch or computer.

3.2 Contacts & Calendar in iCloud

Just like the Mail app, the Contacts and Calendar app are dead-ringers for their iOS and Apple-based brethren. Schedule one appointment or make changes to contact information, and your edits automatically sync to every device, including iCloud.com

Calendar: Unfortunately, iCloud does not support or sync with Google calendars or any WebDAV calendars. So while you can view and edit your Google calendar on your phone, iPad or even the Mac version of iCal, any events you add to a Google or other WebDAV calendar will not be accessible using the iCloud website. You'll only be able to see events directly associated with your iCloud calendar. If you use Apple's iCloud calendar for personal use and also maintain a shared Google calendar at work, the lack of simultaneous access is a definite drawback. However, since it only affects the online version (iCloud.com), this won't be a significant issue for most users.

Contacts: Contact syncing and back up may be one of the best features of iCloud. There's nothing more frustrating than having to add the same contact multiple times to both your iPad, iPhone and email contact list, not to mention losing all your contact data in an untimely phone death. iCloud will automatically push any new contact information you add straight to your other iDevices, as well as the Address Book on your Mac or your Outlook contacts on your PC. No more cables or syncing!

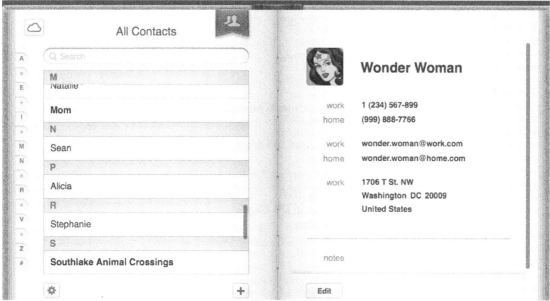

Contacts on iCloud.com

Contacts on iPhone

3.3 Documents in iCloud

Goodbye, iTunes data syncing! Now you can back up and transfer documents via iCloud from your different devices, without syncing your work via iTunes or emailing files between devices. Well, kind of – iCloud makes some big promises for iWork files, although syncing works better across iDevices, rather than between the desktop and an iDevice.

In order to take full advantage of iCloud's document sharing and syncing, you'll need mobile versions of iWork (Pages, Numbers and Keynote) on your iPhone or iPad. Anytime you create or edit a document, the Pages, Numbers and Keynote apps will automatically save changes as you work. These changes are then synced to all your devices, so if you open a document on your iPad, it looks exactly like the document you were just editing on your iPhone (it even opens to the same place).

I started this document on my iPhone.

I started this document on my iPhone.

And it instantly appeared for use on my iPad.

Unfortunately, iCloud's web-based iWork does not integrate well with the full desktop versions of iWork. Rather than having documents "instantly available" as they are on mobile devices, you'll need to upload or download a document to sync with iCloud. Additionally, to edit a document you first created on your iPhone or iPad, you'll need to download it first. While not having to sync your files or presentations via iTunes is a definite plus, you'll still need to download and upload files; there's no 'instant access' like there is on an iDevice. If you do a lot of document editing on the go, iCloud is not yet a replacement for Google Docs or Dropbox.

3.4 Photo Stream

Thanks to Photo Stream, any photo you take with your iPhone can now be viewed instantly on your iPad, Apple TV or on your computer via the iPhoto or Aperture programs. Photos you take on one iDevice are synced to other devices via your iCloud account. There's no need to manually upload or download any images, and emailing photos between your computer and iPhone (or syncing via iTunes) is now a thing of the past. To make the most out of Photo Stream, you'll want to be using an iPhone to shoot your pictures as well as either iPhoto or Aperture on your Mac to edit and save your images. Here's how to get started.

What is Photo Stream?

Photo Stream is an iCloud feature that holds up to 1,000 of your latest photos for up to 30 days. From any iDevice, you can view images in your Photo Stream by going to Photos -> Albums -> Photo Stream.

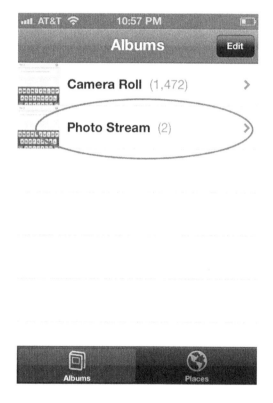

Since images in your Photo Stream don't stick around forever, you will need to permanently add any favorites to your iDevice. To do so, tap the photo and select the 'Save to Camera Roll' option.

You can also import images directly to your computer with Photo Stream in iPhoto or Aperture.

How do I clear my Photo Stream?
By default, you cannot edit or remove a photo from your Photo Stream; iCloud does this automatically after 30 days or when it reaches 1,000 photos, whichever comes first. However, you can reset the entire stream.
1. To do so, go to iCloud.com and click on your user name.
2. Click Advanced and select the 'Reset Photo Stream' button; this will clear your entire Photo Stream.

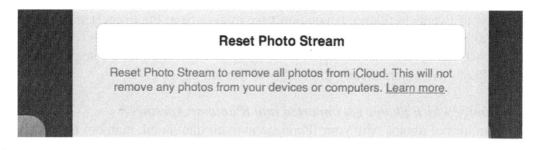

3. Next, you'll need to reset each device's Photo Stream.
4. Go to Settings -> Photos and toggle the Photo Stream option on and off.

How do I enable Photo Stream for iPhoto or Aperture?

1. First, make sure that Photo Stream is enabled for your computer; go to System Preferences -> iCloud and ensure Photo Stream is checked off.
2. Next, enable Photo Stream for your photo app.
3. From either iPhoto or Aperture, go to Preferences -> Photo Stream and select 'Enable Photo Stream'
4. Select 'Automatic Import' to automatically add your Photo Stream photos to your Faces, Places, Photos and Events albums

NOTE: You can't use Photo Stream in both iPhoto and Aperture at the same time. If it's currently enabled in one program and you try to enable it in the other, you'll receive an error message. Since most people use exclusively iPhoto or Aperture, this should not be a conflict.

Why are my Photo Stream photos not importing in iPhoto?

Even with 'Automatic Import' checked under preferences, iPhoto may still need a little kick-start assistance. Here's what to do:

1. Check your Events in iPhoto. If you don't see images from Photo Stream, use the "Add to" button to manually make an album with your Photo Stream images
2. iPhoto will ask if you wish to import these images; select OK and create your album
3. Now, iPhoto will automatically import Photo Stream images

How can I manage which photos get imported into iPhoto or Aperture?

It's easy to snap tons of photos with your iPhone, and in all likelihood, many of these will not be worth keeping. If you don't want to automatically import every image (only to delete hundreds at a later date), turn off iPhoto or Aperture's "Automatic Import" option. You'll still be able to view everything in your Photo Stream, but can pick and choose which images to import.

NOTE: The photos that you import to your computer off your SD card or camera will be automatically added to your Photo Stream. To disable this feature, go to Preferences -> Photo Stream and uncheck the Automatic Upload option.

3.5 Books & Apps

iCloud makes it easy to download books and apps previously purchased through the App Store or the iBookstore onto any iDevice.

How do I see a list of previously purchased apps?
1. From the app store, tap 'Updates' from the bottom menu
2. Tap 'Purchased' at the top of the list; this will launch a list of every app ever purchased using your Apple ID
3. You can switch between viewing a list of all purchased apps (starting with the most

recently purchased app listed first) and apps not currently on your device ("Not On This iPhone")

How do I download an app that I've purchased but is not currently installed on my device?
To download an app not currently on your device, tap the iCloud download icon; your download will instantly begin.

How do I see previously purchased iBooks?
Just like with apps, go to the iBookstore and tap the 'Purchased' icon at the bottom of the screen. A list of all purchased iBooks will appear, along with a sub-list of those iBooks that are currently on your device.

How do I download an iBook that I previously purchased?

Just like with the App Store, tap the iCloud download icon next to the book title; your download will instantly begin.

Can my iBooks sync across devices?
Yes. Just like when reading books through the Amazon Kindle app, any books read using iBooks will sync across all your iDevices. You can start a book on your iPhone and pick right up on your iPad where you left off. Even better, if you have automatic downloads enabled for iBooks, when you leave your iPhone and go to your iPad, your new book will be ready and waiting – you won't even need to download it.

3.6 Find My Friends

Find My Friends is an iCloud feature that lets you share your GPS location with other Find My Friends app users; you choose which friends can see your location. Find My Friends is a convenient app for using at, say, a giant amusement park or outdoor concert where it can be tough to precisely locate someone. Most importantly, you are in complete control over your privacy settings, controlling who sees your location and when (if ever) you share your location. Here's how to get started:

1. You'll need to download the free 'Find My Friends' app for either your iPhone or iPad
2. To add a friend, send a friend request; once your Friend accepts your request, you'll be able to see them on the map
3. To temporarily add a friend for location sharing (like a work group at a conference), select the "Temporary" option from the bottom menu
4. To see your current location, select the "Me" option from the bottom menu
5. To hide your current location from friends, choose Me -> Hide from Followers and toggle this to the ON position; signing out will also disable any location sharing

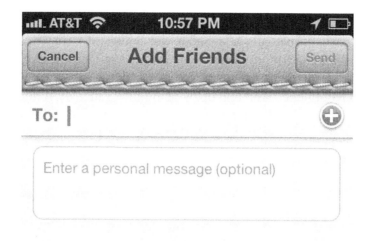

One downside to Find My Friends is that the app only works with a unique Apple ID, so if an entire family shares the same ID for multiple devices, you won't be able to locate anyone.

3.7 Find my iPhone

Find My iPhone is an iCloud feature that allows you to locate your missing iPhone or iPad on a map and remotely lock or erase its contents. When you first set up your iPhone or iPad, you will be prompted to activate this feature. In order for the Find My iPhone app to work, you will also need to activate location services. This allows GPS data from your iPhone or iPad to be used to locate it. Conversely, if you turn off 'Location Services' or are in Airplane mode, the Find My iPhone won't be able to work. Find My iPhone works virtually the same for either an iPhone or iPad.

What happens if I lose my phone?

While our phones may seem perpetually attached to our bodies, it's easy to set the phone down when grabbing coffee, shopping for groceries, or even walking out of a meeting and leaving it on the conference table. If you've misplaced your phone, you can easily track its location by either logging on to the "Find My Phone" web app or by using the "Find My iPhone" app on another phone, your iPad or your iPod Touch. The app will approximate your iPhone's location, so you can head back to the conference room or local coffee shop and pick up your phone.

How can I display a message or play a sound?

If you've located your phone in a public place and are on the way to retrieve it, you can also use the Find My iPhone app to write a message that displays on your screen, such as "This phone is lost, please call me at XXX-XXX-XXXX." What if location services says your phone is right there with you but you can't find it? If your phone is lost under a pile of papers in the office or stuck behind the sofa, you can also use the app to make your phone play a sound to help you locate it, even if your phone setting is on silent.

How do I protect data on a lost phone?

If your phone does not have a passcode lock, you can set one remotely using the Find My iPhone app. If the worst happens and you simply can't track down your phone or assume it has been stolen, you can also initiate a remote data wipe through the Find My iPhone app. This will erase all your data and cannot be undone. As a word of caution, once your data is wiped, your iPhone can no longer be tracked through the Find My iPhone app. However, if you assume it's a lost cause and you don't want your personal information falling into a stranger's hands, wiping the phone is a quick and easy way to protect your privacy. Even better, since your iPhone automatically backs up with iCloud, nothing is lost. If you find your missing phone, you can easily restore your data using iCloud. And worst-case scenario, you can use your iCloud backup to set up a new phone just like your old one.

Section 4: iCloud & iTunes Match

4.1 iTunes in the Cloud: Music

Your music is now in the cloud! Any music you've ever purchased using your Apple ID is now available for download through iCloud.

Just like with books and app purchases, you can browse your music download history, and re-download any songs to any device associated with your Apple ID.

How do I view a list of purchased music?

1. From your computer, open iTunes and launch the iTunes Store
2. Select the "Purchased" option from the Quick Links list on the right
3. You'll see a screen that looks like this, giving you the option to download any music you've purchased:

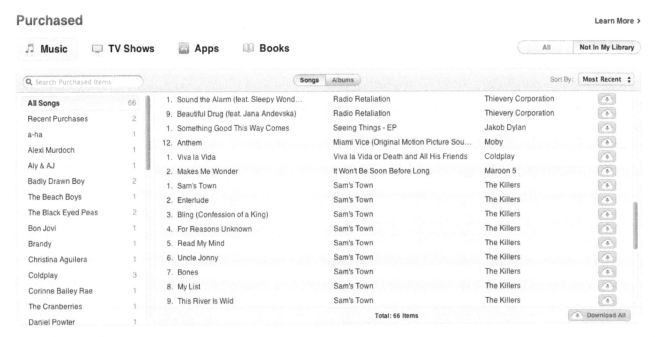

song view mode

Use the top right buttons to toggle between all purchased music and music that is not currently on your computer.

A list on the left of the screen will display quick links to every song purchased, as well as each song organized by artist. In addition to browsing alphabetically, you can see the most recent 50 items purchased from iTunes.

Selecting an artist's name will bring up a listing of every album or partial album you have from that artist. The download screen for an album gives the user the opportunity to download individual songs or the entire album in one action.

You can sort by song or album, and organize by your most recent purchases or the name of the song/album.

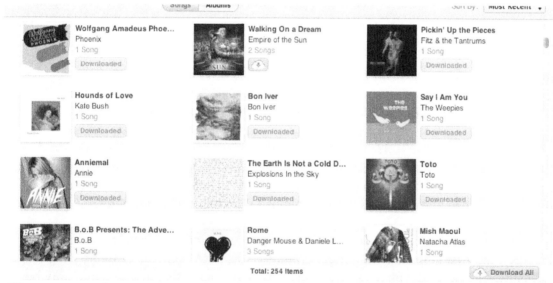

Album view mode

How do I download purchased music on to my device?
If a song is not currently on your device, you'll see a cloud icon with a download arrow. Click the icon to add it to your device. The download will start immediately, and as soon as it's complete, the cloud icon will be replaced by a "Downloaded" button.

4.2. Setting up iTunes Match

iTunes match is a paid service ($24.99/year) that lets users match and upload music to a central cloud server and then access this music anytime, anywhere, from any device. iTunes Match works by scanning all the tracks currently in your iTunes music library. iTunes will then match as many of these tracks as possible with music already in its 20 million+ song library. If iTunes Match finds a song that doesn't match, it will upload this to track the central cloud server, so you'll still be able to stream or download these songs to other devices.

Why use iTunes Match?
For a relatively small price tag ($24.99), iTunes match offers two key services: unlimited storage and instant access/download privileges. First, you'll be able to listen to everything you own wherever you are – and there's no need to manually upload anything. Secondly, once your library is matched up, you'll be able to download any song at any time onto any device in a high-quality, 256-kbps DRM-free AAC files. Those low-quality tracks you ripped from friends in college? They've just been upgraded. This also means that you'll never need to worry about backing up your entire music library again, or even having your entire library on your computer, freeing up valuable memory space.

Is there a limit to how many songs can be matched/uploaded by iTunes Match?
iTunes Match limits the number of songs to 25,000. However, any song purchased through iTunes does not count against this overall total.

Does the Apple ID I use for iTunes Match need to be the same one for my iCloud account?
Nope! You can use whatever ID you'd like for iTunes Match – although whichever one you pick you cannot change for 90 days. This is to prevent people from matching their music library, swapping out IDs, and then allowing a friend to download it all onto their computer.

What if my music library is associated with multiple iTunes accounts and DRM music?
When the iTunes Store first launched, all purchased music was DRM-protected. Every song that was downloaded was associated with a specific Apple ID. This meant that a song could only be played on a computer that was authorized to play music associated with that specific Apple ID. Apple also limited the total number of authorized devices per Apple ID to five. So if you wanted to play your music at work and at home, and your spouse also wanted access, you could very quickly hit your five-device limit. In fact, most people have music libraries filled with songs that have been purchased using multiple Apple IDs. iTunes Match is finally putting an end to the chaos. When iTunes Match scans your library, it will match any and all songs authorized to play on your computer, regardless of the Apple ID associated with the song. This means that after your library is matched, you'll be able to download 256-kbps DRM-free AAC files of all your rights-managed songs.

What is the difference between matching and uploading tracks?

Apple has a library with over 20 million songs. This means that the majority of your songs will be matched to existing titles in this library. If a song does not match, Apple will upload your version as-is to the server for playback.

How do I know if a song is matched or uploaded?

In order to determine if a song has been matched or uploaded, turn on the iCloud Download and iCloud Status columns. From iTunes, go to View -> View Options. The iCloud Status column will let you know how your tracks have been labeled (matched or uploaded) by iTunes Match.

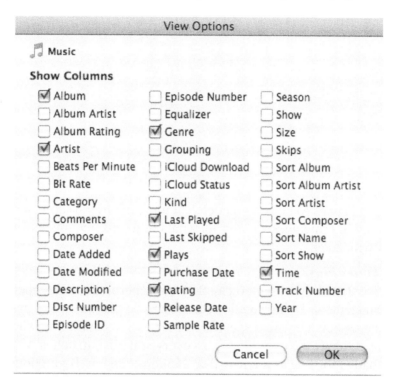

Select iCloud Download and iCloud Status to see whether a song is matched or uploaded

How do I upgrade my low-quality tracks?

Once iTunes Match has scanned your entire library, you can delete your low quality tracks and download new, 256kbps AAC quality tracks. For a quick way of identifying all the tracks in need of an upgrade, build a Smart Playlist.

NOTE: As a word of caution, prior to deleting your tracks, be sure to back up your library to an external drive.

1. Go to File -> New Smart Playlist
2. Add the following rules: "Bit Rate is less than 256 kbps" and "Media Kind is music"
3. Option click on the "+" icon to add a conditional rule: "Any" of the following are true
4. Add the following optional rules: "iCloud Status is Matched" and "iCloud Status is

Purchased"
5. You can now delete all the songs on your Smart Playlist, and download new versions from iTunes Match.

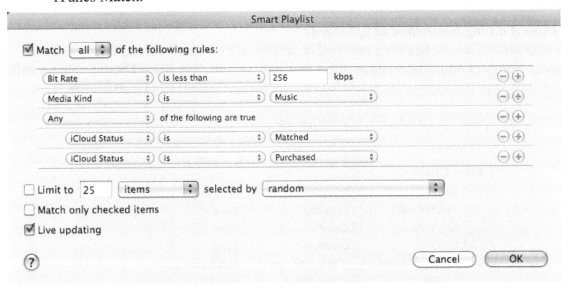

Thanks to the beauty of iTunes Match, if you delete a track in order to download a higher-quality version, iTunes Match will remember all your metadata (e.g., play counts, ratings, tags, etc.) when the new version is downloaded.

What happened to iTunes Plus?

iTunes Plus is a service that allows users to pay 0.30 cents per track to free their music from the shackles of rights management. Doing so allows a song to be played on any machine or device – it no longer needed to be associated with a specific iTunes user account. For iTunes Match users, there's no longer a need to pay the upgrade fee, as every song that matches with the iTunes virtual library can be downloaded for free as a DRM-free 256kbps version. If you don't use iTunes Match, you can still upgrade individual songs with iTunes Plus.

Is there any music that iTunes Match can't match?

According to Apple, iTunes Match won't be able to match files over 200MB, DRM songs that you are not authorized to play and DRM songs purchased from a non-U.S. iTunes store (although that last restriction should change when iTunes Match becomes available to international subscribers). Additionally, you won't be able to match any music less than 96kbps. However, you may be able to work around this restriction by upgrading the quality of your track. From iTunes, go to Advanced -> Create AAC version. For a quick way to identify all tracks in need of AAC conversion, build a Smart Playlist.

What about pirated music – will I get in trouble for having illegal music on my computer?

Most of us have a few tracks from the old days of Napster, Kazaa and other peer-to-peer sharing networks. However, it seems unlikely that Apple will know whether a specific track was legitimately obtained or not when it matches your music. It's also likely that part of the $24.99/year fee goes to placating the record companies. If you're concerned about getting busted for piracy, simply convert your songs to AAC versions as described above (Advanced -> Create AAC version).

What if all my music was purchased through iTunes – do I need iTunes Match?
Nope! You can already enjoy all the benefits of iTunes Match for free via iCloud.

4.3 Using iTunes Match: Mac, PC and iOS devices

Now that iTunes Match is set up and your tracks are upgraded, you can enjoy having access to all your music anywhere you go.

How do I activate iTunes Match on my iOS device?
From any iPhone, iPod Touch or iPad, go to Settings -> Music and toggle the "iTunes Match" option to ON. You'll need to enter the Apple ID associated with your iTunes Match account.

How does iTunes Match work with my computer and iOS devices?
On a computer, any songs stored in the cloud (and not currently on your computer's hard drive) will be played will be streamed. You also have the option to download these songs directly on to your computer by clicking the iCloud button. Even if you are not an iTunes Match user, you'll notice this stream/download option is currently available for all music you have purchased through iTunes. To see these tracks, go to the iTunes Store and select the "Purchased" option from the Quick Links list on the right. You'll see a screen that gives you the option to download any music you've purchased.

On your iOS device, iTunes requires that you download the track prior to listening to it; streaming is not an option. You'll be able to start listening to the track as soon as the download begins. Since Apple TVs lack storage capacity, you'll only be able to stream music.

Are my playlists also available on all my devices?
Yes. Your playlists will also sync across all your devices, meaning if you create, edit, or delete a playlist on your iPhone, the same list will be automatically updated on your Mac or PC. Even better, if you play a song on your iPad and then open iTunes on your computer, you'll notice that the song's play count has automatically increased.

How do I manage what music is available on my devices?

If you've got a library with 10,000 songs, the last thing you want to do is download every song on to your iPhone. In fact, you don't even have to see every song on your current playlist. From your iOS device (iPhone, iPod Touch and iPad), go to Settings -> Music and toggle off the "Show All Music" option. Now your playlists will only display songs currently downloaded on your iOS device. The option to download additional songs still exits, even though your extensive music library will just be "hidden" from view.

If I delete a song from my iPhone, will it also be deleted from my computer?
No. If you delete a song from you music library on any iDevice, the song will continue to live on your computer. However, if you remove a song from a playlist on one device, it will be removed from the same playlist on all devices (although the song itself will continue to exist on all your devices.) iTunes Match syncs information (play counts, metadata, playlists) across devices, but gives you the option to individually manage which songs are downloaded onto which devices.

Does iTunes Match know when I add a song to my computer?
Yes! Periodically iTunes Match will scan for new music. You can also manually tell iTunes to do a force refresh by going Store -> Update iTunes Match. Run into a problem with a specific song? From within iTunes, right click on the track and select the "Add to iCloud" option.

Can I transfer my music library from one computer to another using iTunes Match?
If both computers are yours (and associated with the same Apple ID), then the answer is yes. In theory, you can download your entire music library onto another computer from the cloud. However, depending on the size of your music library this could be a lengthy undertaking, even with the speediest of Internet connections. Backing up and exporting your music library through iTunes may be the best option.

Can I use iTunes Match on my computer but not on my iOS device?
Of course! Simply keep the "iTunes Match" option toggled off on your iOS device. You can still sync your iOS device as you normally would with your computer.

What if I decide to cancel iTunes Match after the first year – will I lose my upgraded music?
Nope! All those songs that you upgraded to a DRM-free 256kbps version will continue to work and are yours to keep. You will, however, lose all the cloud storage as well we your ability to sync playlists and non-iTunes purchased music across all your devices.

Is iTunes Match worth the $24.99?
In our opinion, iTunes Match is definitely worth the $24.99, especially if you have a large music library. The ability to access any song at any time simply can't be beat. Additionally, if you have a lot of music that you rarely listen to, but you still want instant access to all of it (i.e., you don't want to have to connect an external drive and hunt for a specific song to add it back to your machine), iTunes Match is an invaluable space saver. Finally, iTunes Match is a great way to "free" your DRM music, especially those songs that were purchased using a friend or family member's Apple ID. By matching and downloading non-protected versions, you can finally take your music wherever you want it to go – sans Apple's pesky five-computer authorization limit.

However, if the majority of your music was purchased through iTunes (rather than burned from CDs or obtained via friends), then enough of your songs may already be available via iCloud for free so that iTunes Match just doesn't make sense for your listening habits. For the relatively low price tag, however, it's definitely worth trying out the service.

Section 5: iCloud Accounts & Backup

5.1 iCloud Accounts

How do I set up or change my iCloud account?
Your iCloud account is the Apple ID associated with all your iDevices. In order to sync content across your devices, each one will need to be associated with the same Apple ID. This can be separate from the ID that you use to purchase music, but must be the same for every iDevice and computer.

Can I change my iCloud account?
You are free to change an iCloud account associated with a device at any time. Note, however, that changing the iCloud account may cause the loss of data associated with that specific account.

5.2 iCloud Backup

iCloud backup may quite possible be the most important and significant feature to be included with iCloud. Once every day, iCloud automatically backs up any iDevice (iPod Touch, iPhone or iPad) when it is connected to a Wi-Fi network and plugged in to a power source. Backup happens nearly instantly, and most users will never be aware that backup is even occurring. What does this mean for you? In the event your iPhone is lost or stolen, your data is securely protected (via the 'Find My iPhone' app) and can be instantly retrieved and added to a replacement iPhone via iCloud backup. All your photos, settings, apps and personal data will be right there for you, just like nothing ever happened.

What does iCloud backup?
Purchased music, TV shows, apps and books
Photos and videos in Camera Roll
Device Settings
App data
Home screen and app organization
Messages (iMessage, SMS and MMS)
Ringtones

How much room is available for backup?
Every Apple ID account receives 5GB of free space for backup. Any purchased music, apps, books, TV shows, iTunes match, and Photo Stream content do not count against the free 5GB. Many users will find that this storage allotment is more than enough for email, documents, Camera Roll, account information, etc.

How do I control what is backed up?

Go to Settings -> iCloud and select the "Storage & Backup" option from the bottom of the iCloud settings menu. You'll see a breakdown of how much storage you have in total and current available storage. Tap the "Manage Storage" option for further information and select your device. From here you'll see a list of the latest backup, the backup size, and backup options for each different app.

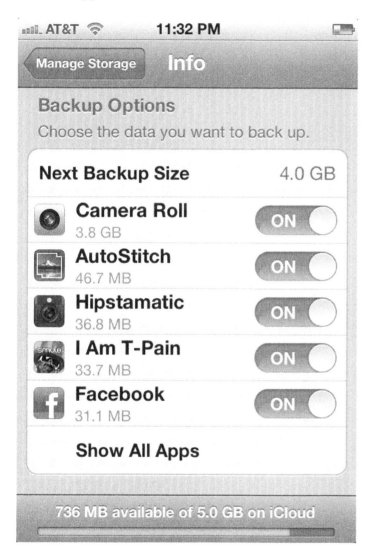

For example, in the screenshot above, it's easy to see that the Camera Roll is taking up the vast majority of the backup space due to a high number of video clips on the camera. Once you've identified the reason why your backup is nearly out of space, you can either disable backup of the app all together (using the ON/OFF toggle switch), or manually remove data from the offending app. In this case, removing some of the videos from the Camera Roll (which had already been synced with a computer, thanks to Photo Stream) will free up space for the backup. It's very rare that additional backup space will need to be purchased, even if it appears that your storage is full.

Can I purchase more backup space?

Out of room? If you need a storage upgrade, you can purchase an additional 10GB for $20/year, 20GB for $40/year and 50GB for $100/year. You can make this purchase directly from any iDevice by going to Settings -> iCloud -> Storage & Backup -> Buy More Storage.

Section 6: Conclusion

For a free service, iCloud offers a number of benefits, although for diehard Apple fans, there are some gaping holes. While iCloud works right out of the box, fine-tuning your preferences (yes, sync my contacts, no, don't automatically download my entire Photo Steam into Aperture) is essential for getting the most out of the service. In fact, between all the different system preferences (and multiple iDevices you may own), you may find that you need to devote a fair amount of time to initial setup and customization. iCloud may not be Apple' most elegant system, but once you've got it set up to your specifications, you can step back and let it do its thing – no extra monitoring required.

For a free, online media storage solution, iCloud, along with iTunes Match, is great for music. When it comes to document transfer, however, iCloud is not quite magical. It duplicates a lot of what MobileMe already did, although by bundling these services with iDevices for free, it expands them to a much larger audience than MobileMe ever reached. However, for efficient document access and transfer, Dropbox (with its iPhone and iPad apps) and Google Documents still beats out iCloud.

As you start using iCloud, you may notice some other frustrating drawbacks, many of which we have addressed in this guide. Why can't all your current calendars sync with Apple's iCalendar? How come editing documents between the iPhone and iPad is seamless, but a complete hassle when it comes to returning to the desktop or even iWork.com? And seriously, what's up with Photo Stream syncing every one of your photos by default? (Just be careful not to take any salacious snaps on your iPhone – and have them end up on your work computer when Photo Stream does its 'auto-syncing'!) Other features, like Find My Friends, may seem like a good idea in theory, but fall short in execution. Learning to make the most of iCloud, however, will help you work around these frustrations and customize iCloud to make it work for your needs.

And while iCloud may not be perfect, there's great comfort in knowing that should something go wrong (be it a stolen iPad or broken iPhone) all your data is right where you need it – in the Cloud. You'll be able to restore all your settings and data on a new iPhone or iPad, creating a clone of your former iDevice (sans the cracked screen). In our busy lives, automatic syncing and updating is a huge plus, especially because it's difficult to remember to back an iPhone up every day (or even once a week).

iCloud may not be perfect, but it's an exciting step forward for instant access to information on all our devices. And with a little tweaking (as suggested in this guide), you can really get the most of this free service.

About Minute Help Press

Minute Help Press is building a library of books for people with only minutes to spare. Follow @minutehelp on Twitter to receive the latest information about free and paid publications from Minute Help Press, or visit minutehelp.com.

CPSIA information can be obtained at www.ICGtesting.com
Printed in the USA
LVOW03s0852081213

364355LV00001B/4/P